Children Writing For Children • Children Writing For Children • Children Writing For Children • Children Writing Fc

Children Writing For Children • Children Writing For Children • Children Writing For Children • Children Writing F

Children Writing For Children • Children Writing For Children • Children Writing For Children • Children Writing F

Children Writing For Children • Children Writing For Children • Children Writing For Children • Children Writing F

D1309287

HILLARY'S
Book Of
A B C's

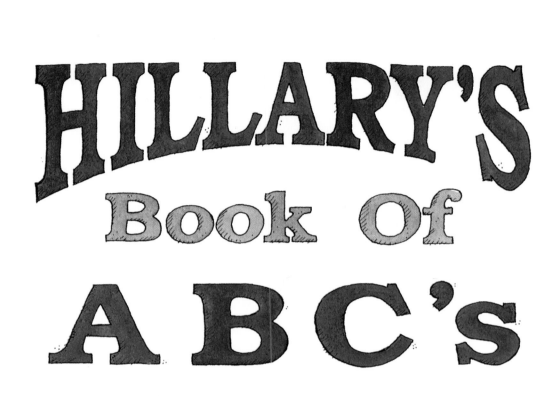

Written & Illustrated by
KAITLIN RASBURRY

CHILDREN WRITING FOR CHILDREN

RASPBERRY PUBLICATIONS

DEDICATION

For All My Teachers Who Taught Me The Joys of Learning To Read and Write.

– Kaitlin Rasburry

Special Thanks to:

Graphic Design
Richard Jenks

Parent Guide
Rachel Rasburry

Reader Response
Joan Grundey
Susan Holland

Printed in Mexico
The stories, characters, and/or incidents in this publication are entirely fictional.

FIRST EDITION   ISBN: 1-884825-00-1

RASPBERRY PUBLICATIONS

Presents...

HILLARY'S
Book Of
A B C's

A n **a**lligator **a**te **a**pples **a**ll **a**fternoon

B ob brought blue balloons to the birthday bash.

C

A curious cat
crept cautiously.

Dozens of dalmations danced downtown.

E ight **e**normous **e**lephants **e**ntered the **e**levator.

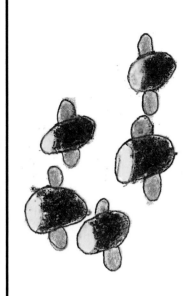

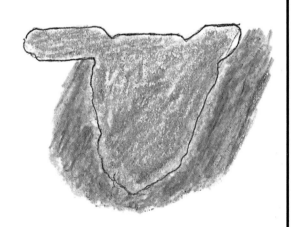

F ive fluttering fireflys flew
from Florida.

G ertrude **g**oat **g**razed **g**ently on the **g**reen **g**rass.

H undreds of happy hippos hurried home.

Irene and Iris insisted on ice cream.

J onathon juggled jugs
of jelly beans.

K
aitlin knows kindergarten kids.

L ions and leopards leaped
over loads of laundry.

Mrs. Monkey made muffins Monday morning.

N ine nieces needed new necklaces and nightgowns.

One octopus offering an oyster omelet.

P
retty **p**ink **p**igs **p**layed **p**olitely with **p**orcupines

Quails quacked quietly
on a quilt.

R ed razorbacks raced running rabbits.

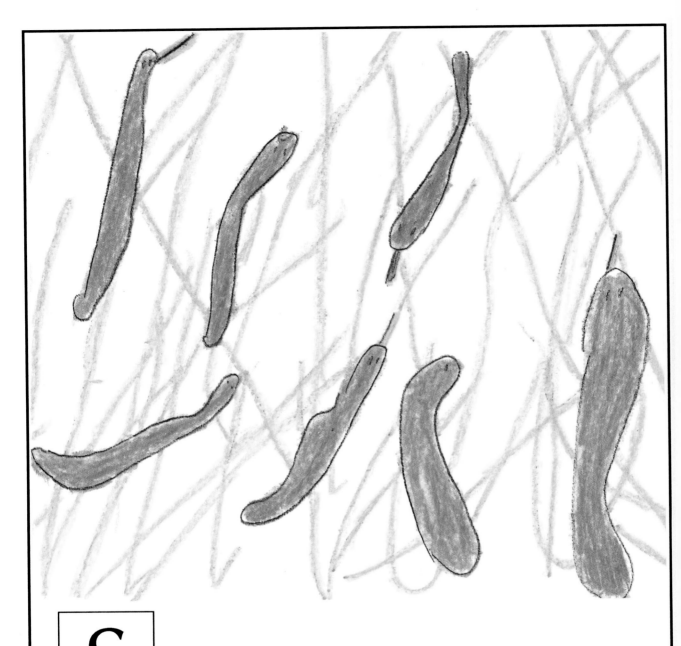

S even silly snakes slithered swiftly southward.

T errible **tigers** tossed
tomatoes **to** ten **turtles.**

U

Uncle Ulmer played the **u**kelele **u**nder an **u**mbrella.

V ictor played violin in a velvet vest.

W ally Walrus walked west
to Washington for waffles.

X

A fox in sox loves to
box and eat lox.

Y A **young yellow yak yodeled** in Yellowstone.

$\boxed{\text{Z}}$ any **zebras zipped** through **zinnias.**

Other Publications By Kaitlin Rasburry

A Monster in My Mouth

Two fears all children have are of the unknown and being different from other children. *A Monster in My Mouth* addresses these fears with an authentic voice. Kaitlin uses a positive attitude and her natural curiosity to overcome her fear of the dentist and her new retainer. This multi-cultural narrative provides a fun and useful tale which will help other children get through this frightful, yet common, experience.

The Cat Sat

A delightful method book to teach short and long vowel sounds. It has a rhythm that makes it as much fun to hear as it is to read. This multi-cultural book will encourage young readers, not only to learn these sounds by words, but also to create examples of their own. A humorous and fun way to get children involved in learning to read.

Publishers Directory

More than 40 listings of publishers who are serious about accepting children's manuscripts. An excellent resource tool for libraries and young serious writers.

Order Information

Call Toll Free 1-800-759-7171 or Mail check or money order to:
RASPBERRY PUBLICATIONS, Inc.
P.O. Box 925 • Westerville, OH 43081-9998

HILLARY'S BOOK OF ABC's	**$14.95**
THE CAT SAT	**$14.95**
A MONSTER IN MY MOUTH	**$14.95**
Publishers Directory of Children's Manuscripts	**$ 8.95**

Shipping $3.50 for first book & 50¢ each additional item.
Ohio residents add 5.75% sales tax .

Parent Guide
–Beginning Exercise

– The first shared reading should be a time to discover the book, the characters, and the illustrations. By demonstrating your interest and enthusiasm through reading, you will model for your child what an *enjoyable* experience books can provide. When the first reading of books are fun, they can lead to years of positive identification with books yet to be discovered by your child.

– Later, reread the story taking time to point at the words so your child will soon attach meaning to words in print and develop an understanding of left-right progression.

– After you have shared the story several times, encourage your child to participate. Leave out words and let your child fill-in. **PRAISE APPROXIMATIONS!** Point out illustrations and have your child locate the corresponding word on the page. This activity can be done time and time again. Repetition is essential for learning and don't forget to make it *fun* for the best learning experience possible.

–Extension Activities

– Help your child develop his/her own alphabet book using the basic story structure.

– Make alphabet letters with play dough.

– Recycle a discarded coffee can and turn it into a letter can. Pick a letter from the alphabet and fill the can with things that start with that letter.

– Experiment with magnetic alphabet letters and a cookie sheet. Practice making words from the story.

– Create an alphabet collage with letter stamps and an ink pad. (Use a fruit scented ink pad!)

– Cut some words from a magazine and put in alphabetical order. Use them to make a child's first dictionary!!

–Most Important

– The value is in *playing* with the book. Don't use it so much as a learning tool, but as a time to share with your child that will be perceived and realized as *pleasurable*.

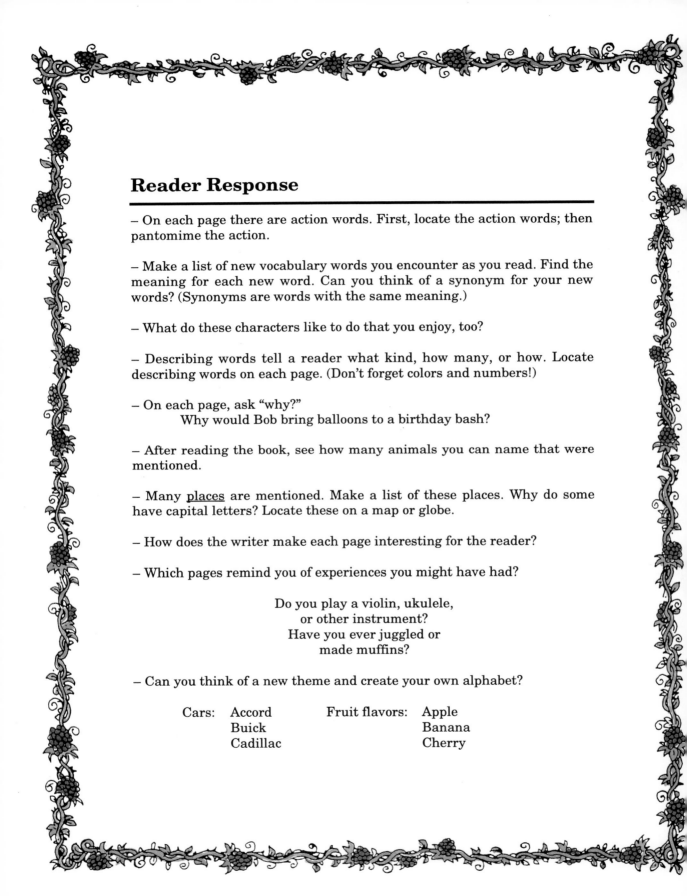

Reader Response

– On each page there are action words. First, locate the action words; then pantomime the action.

– Make a list of new vocabulary words you encounter as you read. Find the meaning for each new word. Can you think of a synonym for your new words? (Synonyms are words with the same meaning.)

– What do these characters like to do that you enjoy, too?

– Describing words tell a reader what kind, how many, or how. Locate describing words on each page. (Don't forget colors and numbers!)

– On each page, ask "why?"
      Why would Bob bring balloons to a birthday bash?

– After reading the book, see how many animals you can name that were mentioned.

– Many <u>places</u> are mentioned. Make a list of these places. Why do some have capital letters? Locate these on a map or globe.

– How does the writer make each page interesting for the reader?

– Which pages remind you of experiences you might have had?

Do you play a violin, ukulele,
or other instrument?
Have you ever juggled or
made muffins?

– Can you think of a new theme and create your own alphabet?

Cars:	Accord	Fruit flavors:	Apple
	Buick		Banana
	Cadillac		Cherry